IREL

Published by Magna Books
Magna Road
Wigston
Leicester LE8 2ZH

Produced by Bison Books Ltd
Kimbolton House
117A Fulham Rd.
London SW3 6RL

ISBN 1-85422-044-6

Printed in Hong Kong

AND

JONAH SULLIVAN

N

RAN BARNES

MAGNA BOOKS

assume them. These clans were called Aithechthuatha, meaning the lower clans. These clans were comprised under the general title of Feni an old Irish word which became Fianna in Middle Irish. The Fianna were a permanent fighting force, which was paid for by a levy on subjects. Finn mac Coul, the hero of the Fianna, belonged to an Aithechthuatha of Leinster. Leinster was one of the new overlords after whose family one of the provinces of Ireland is named. Among the subject or rent-paying peoples of Ireland archeological sources reveal a tribe called the Erainn, who gave their name to Ireland. Ireland is also called Eire, in Old Irish Eriu. The Irish Erenn were the Iverni, whom the Roman historian Ptolemy places in the south west. This tribe also appears on the Celtic lists as living in the district of Luachair, covering the north of Kerry and the adjacent parts of Limerick and Cork. Here was situated Teamhar Erann, that is Tara of the Erainn, which had been the chief burial-ground and meeting-place of the Erainn before it became one of the religious centers of Munster. It is also possible to find the traces of the tribe in Connaught and in Leinster, scattered remnants of an ancient population, driven by invaders into corners where they tried to make a stand. The early Irish Christians were consumed by a curiosity to find out about what happened in their country before the dawn of documented history. In the eleventh and twelfth centuries an effort was made in the *Book of Invasions* to reconstruct the succession of the different peoples who were considered to have invaded the country in prehistoric times. Despite the strength of the oral tradition in Ireland, the work of these early historians cannot be taken literally, for the events supposed to have taken place are alleged to have taken place some 1000 years before they were written down. Furthermore, these historians had patrons who wanted their lineage and family heroics to be traced just as much as they wanted a history of Ireland to be written.

Politically the history of Ireland is overshadowed by the Catholic Church and by the British state, whether headed by King or by Government, and many would avow that these two influences still loom largest of all in the historical influences today. Henry VIII assumed the title 'King of Ireland,' in 1541. This title had been a lordship of the English Crown since the conquest of the twelfth century, and it was with the Tudors that the colonization of Ireland thus began. Modern Irish history begins at about this time, the change in the English title signifying prophetically the new policy of total rule by the Tudors. The religious divisions which still play their part in modern Irish politics have obviously got their roots in the division of the Church in the reign of Henry VIII but the issue did not become clearly defined until the reign of Elizabeth I. Her government imposed an Irish church settlement on the English model and was based on the Acts of Supremacy and uniformity also passed by her puppet government in Dublin. The tenets of this act were not imposed with particular force, even within the Pale. So much so that those who refused to take the Act of Supremacy were rarely disturbed by her majesty's officials as long as their political loyalty could be counted on, and some recusants, ie those who refused the oath, were allowed to hold municipal office, some even sitting as judges. For the reason of its paranoia about Spanish influences, England, even though it did not want to involve itself in heavy financial commitment, did concern itself with policies of expansion of royal power in Munster. This province was after all geographically speaking in greatest danger of involvement with Spain. The insurrection in 1569 and that of 1579 which was provided with men, arms and money from Spain proved that England could not be too careful. Elizabeth resolved on a settlement or colony for Munster of English settlers. This project would have a twofold benefit in the eyes of the English: it was cheap, the land that the settlers were to be given would needless to say, not be purchased but taken from its original Irish owners; and it would give England an in situ community of loyal Protestant farmers. The Scottish planters of the seventeenth century were different, possessed of strength and identity which has survived many centuries and survives still. These planters took control of the lands of the Earls and created modern, model towns and a thriving local economy.

The history of Ireland has been dominated for centuries by the struggle with Britain. The nationalist leader, Padraig Pearse, proclaimed, only a few months before his execution for leading the 1916 Rising in Dublin, in words used today by Sinn Fein: 'Ireland unfree shall never be at peace.' After the rebellion and the ensuing War of Independence, David Lloyd George tried again to pacify Ireland, this time by a treaty with the Nationalist leaders which accepted Irish partition, that is the separation from the rest of Ireland of those counties that had been identified as being predominantly Protestant, 'the six counties' and limited independence to a 'Free State' of 26 counties. It was agreed to by Irish representatives, elected as representatives of the nascent Irish government first convened in the Dail of 21 January 1919. In 1919 Sinn Fein set up their own Parliament, Dail Eireann, in Dublin and declared an Irish Republic, headed by Eamon De Valera. The organization that had waged guerrilla warfare on the British now wished to set up a real Government for Ireland. The War of Independence started, ending in a truce in 1921. The northern six counties of Ireland, now named Northern Ireland or, inaccurately, Ulster, accepted secession. Dublin Castle under the British had carefully planned for the eventuality of a separate Northern Ireland, and the British Government created a new post in 1920: the Under Secretary for Ulster. The stage, administratively and politically, had been set for a Belfast Government even before the Government of Ireland Act and long before the Treaty. Thus the Treaty of 1921 did not enable Partition to take place as it is commonly assumed: Partition cleared the way for the Treaty. The 1921 elections were held in Northern Ireland and the Unionist majority was total. What was inaugurated in these six counties of Ulster was, effectively, a one-party state, to the horror of one third of its population, the Catholics. The last political and administrative break was made with Britain in 1937 when the Dail approved a new constitution which carried no reference to the Crown. At the onset of World War II Ireland had been given control of the three ports kept by Britain as part of the Treaty, thus she was in a position where neutrality was possible. Ireland remained neutral during World War II: De Valera was at the time engaging in an internal war against the IRA with whom Fianna Fail and all the official parties had severed links.

Emigration has become in the 1980s and 1990s as real a problem as it was in the grim 1950s. The emigrés this time are quite different from last. It is a sad tribute to the excellence and openness of the education system in Ireland that many of the new emigrants are not navvies but professional, well-educated, young people. Destinations include the USA, with its generous allocation of visas and readiness to take a lot of these people on, Europe and a Britain that does not ever acknowledge the contribution they make and have always made to its wealth and strength. But these are new days and hopefully the Irish abroad will be allowed this time to vaunt their nationality with pride. The link between the United States and Ireland is one of blood, reiterated implicity in the speech of President John Fitzgerald Kennedy on arrival at Dublin Airport 27 July 1963: 'No country in the world, in the history of the world, has endured the haemorrhage which this island has endured over a period of a few years for so many of its sons and daughters. These sons and daughters scattered throughout the world and they give this small island a family of million upon millions in a sense. All of them who visit Ireland come home.'

CONNAUGHT

The western province of Connaught is the most remote and desolate of the four provinces of Ireland. Throughout the centuries its uninviting shoreline and relatively infertile land deterred many invaders. In the ninth century the Vikings entered the eastern part of Ireland but made few attempts to conquer the northwest, and the Anglo-Normans in the twelfth century were also inclined to leave the tribes of Connaught largely to themselves. A happy result of this relative isolation has been the survival in Connaught of the largest areas of Irish-speaking people. Galway, in particular, is a center for Irish cultural and literary studies and is home to the Gaelic League.

Connaught is a province dominated by water. Lakes, rivers, streams, and bogs abound, and the last provide the peat or 'turf,' an important source of fuel. It is cut into bricks and stacked to dry by the waterlogged pits where it is dug. Turf is used not only for domestic heating but also to fire power stations. This watery landscape provided inspiration for Ireland's most distinguished poet, W B Yeats, who spent boyhood holidays at Lough Gill in County Sligo. 'The Lake Isle of Innisfree' recalls an imaginary idyll in Connaught. Rising dramatically above the lakelands of Connaught are many mountains, among them Knocknarra in the west. On its summit is a gigantic cairn, supposedly the tomb of the legendary Queen Maeve, a first-century ruler of Connaught. A fine day affords from it magnificent views to the Ox Mountains to the south and the mountains of Donegal to the north.

There is a sense of freedom in Connaught's wild countryside, and an exhilaration gained from high mountains and long fjord-like valleys and vast moorland bogs. Small villages nestle here and there, farmhouses are scattered around, and stone-built towns like Clifden in the heart of Connemara have a traditional charm. In Killary harbor sheep come down from the mountains to nibble seaweed at low tide. It is a region that retains its traditions, its people are warm and welcoming, and life proceeds at a leisurely and civilized pace while the modern world rushes by.

15 The Maamturk Mountains, Co. Galway, bound one side of the Maam Valley. Leckavrea, the highest in the range is a popular, if difficult climb. The whole of the Maam Valley is in an area of Connemara known unofficially as Joyce's Country which derives its name from a Welsh family who moved here in the thirteenth centry.

16/17 Clifden, Co. Galway. A view from the appropriately named Sky Road overlooking the seaside town of Clifden, which some would call the capital of Connemara. The Twelve Pins are in the background.

18 Bunacuneen, above Maam, Connemara, Co. Galway, is one of the Corcogemore range of mountains which with the Maamturks bounds the Maam Valley.

19 Doo Lough, Co. Mayo. North of the Mweelrea
mountains the Bundorragha river feeds into Doo
Lough, north of Killary Harbour, the longest sea
inlet in Ireland.

20/21 Twelve Pins from Mweelrea, the highest peak in Connemara, which gives a spectacular view over the Twelve Pins or Benna Beola.

22/23 Ben Bulben, Co. Sligo, under which W B Yeats wanted to be buried:
Under bare Ben Bulben's head . . .
By the road an ancient cross
No marble, no conventional phrase,
On limestone quarried near the spot
By his command these words were cut:
Cast a cold eye
On life, on death
Horseman, pass by!

24/25 Kylemore Lake, Co. Galway, the lake, said by locals to be bottomless, where a previous occupant of the Abbey, displeased with the appointments of the interior, threw several tons of Italian marble.

26 MacDonoughs pub, Uachtar Ard, Co. Galway. Uachtar Ard, a pleasant nineteenth-century fishing village, is one of the gateways to Connemara and many fishing, climbing, walking, and sightseeing holidays begin here.

27 Pony and Trap, Inishmore, Aran Islands. There are more motor bikes than cars on the Aran Islands, and some residents still use the donkey and cart as their means of transporting turf (peat for burning) and other staples of life. During the fifth century St Enda received the descendants into the church, starting a monastic tradition which has left the Arans with one of the richest collections of ecclesiastical remains in the country.

28/29 Long Walk and the Spanish Arch, Galway.
A charming row of nineteen-century houses faces
on the Galway Quays and the Claddagh, or old
fishing quarter. Galway, City of the Tribes, is pos-
sibly Ireland's most attractive town. It has many
relics of its historic past which can be traced back
to The Annals of the Four Masters which speak of
it as a port which was the cause of wars between
the kings of Connaught and Munster.

30/31 Naturalized Yucca at Roundstone, Co. Galway, a village which takes its name from a mis-
conception: the name of the village in Irish is
Cloch an Ruan, Seal's rock; when the name was
anglicized it became Roundstone.

32/33 Twelve Pins and Derryclare Lough in
winter.

34/35 Dún Aengus, Inishmore, on the largest of the Aran Islands, a group of three situated between counties Clare and Galway in the mouth of Galway Bay. The remarkable fort which has been described as 'the most magnificent barbaric monument extant in Europe,' is situated on a hill which rises steeply from the sea to a height of 300 feet. It has three lines of ramparts and traces of a fourth which terminate at both ends on the verge of the cliffs.

36/37 The Killaries from Renvyle, Co. Mayo.

38/39 Statue near Kylemore Abbey, Co. Galway.
Statues and shrines abound all over Ireland. In-
terestingly they often lie on the site of episodes
from the folk tales of the pre christian era.

40/41 Stone Beach near Mulranney, Co. Mayo.

ULSTER

The tale of violence over the last twenty years in Ulster has been spread worldwide by television and newspaper. This image of conflict conceals both the age and complexity of the situation in the north, and the beauty of the countryside, from the wild Atlantic coast of Donegal to the gentle green swathes of the nine glens of Antrim.

Unlike today, the north of Ireland was, until the arrival of the Tudors in the sixteenth century, the part of the country most isolated from Britain, little touched by the Anglo-Normans who had colonized and integrated into the rest of Ireland since the twelfth century. In an effort to protect England from Spanish attack, Elizabeth I, and later James VI and I, began to transplant thousands of loyal British farmers to Ulster land, confiscated from its owners. Over the years Catholics were deprived of their civil rights and any access to political or economic power. This led, understandably, to resentment and violence. Although Catholics have now long enjoyed the same political rights as Protestants in the north, there is still a deep-seated resentment at rule from Westminster, while there is an equally profound fear among Protestants of rule from Dublin. Although, ultimately, reunification of Ireland would seem to be the most equable solution to the 'problem of the north,' the opposition of Northern Ireland's Protestants, who would become a minority in the new Ireland, will be fierce.

The fact that Ulster has been the focus of such contention is due in no small part to the rich fertility of its land. The green central lowlands, punctuated by lakes and rivers, are ideal farming country and the ample water power also helped the development of the world-famous linen industry. Belfast, unlike Dublin, has a relatively short history. The city developed from a village in the seventeenth century to its present size through the growth of such industries as cotton, ropemaking, engineering and tobacco. Despite the troubles and consequent economic difficulties, Belfast's industries account for the relative prosperity of the province compared to the rest of Ireland.

43 Greencastle, Foyle Fisheries, Co. Donegal. In the days of massive Irish emigration, many people saw their last view of Ireland from a liner leaving this port.

44/45 Carrick-a-Rede rope bridge, east of Ballin-
toy, Co. Antrim. The prospect of this flimsy struc-
ture is daunting to the visitor.

46 Hamilton's Bawn. A traditional whitewashed cottage in Co. Armagh.

47 Greencastle Castle, Co. Donegal. Richard de
Burgo, the Red Earl of Ulster, erected a strong
Norman castle to overawe the O'Donnells of
Tyrconnell and the other great northern chiefs.
The ruins are extensive.

48/49 Glenarm, Linford Water, and the entrance to Glenarm Castle, Co. Antrim. Chiefly famous for its extensive and beautiful grounds, the building itself has been extensively altered over the years. Over the gateway to the castle is contained the inscription 'With the leave of God this Castle was built by Sir Randle McDonnell, Knight, Erle of Antrim, having to his wife Dame Aellis O'Nill in the year of our God 1636 Deus est adjutor meus.'

*50 Orange Day Parade, Belfast. On July 12th
Ulster Unionists celebrate the Battle of the Boyne,
symbol of British rule in Ireland.*

*51 Loyalist Mural, Coleraine, Co. Derry. A recur-
ring image in loyalist murals is that of William of
Orange, or King Billy, who won the Battle of the
Boyne, champion of Protestant Ulster.*

54 Moville, Co. Donegal. Fishing nets drying at the harbor.

55 Enniskillen Castle, Co. Fermanagh. This castle contains part of the castle built by the Maguires, the chiefs of Fermanagh, in 1439, as well as a late sixteenth-century water gate.

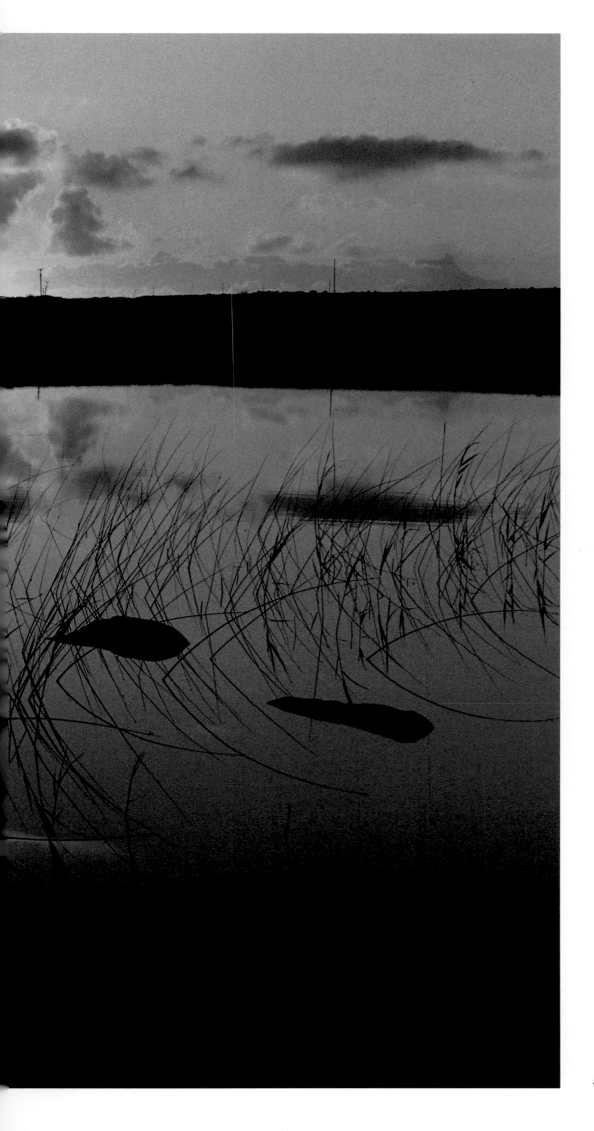

56/57 Near Gweedore, Co. Donegal.

58 Crown Bar, Belfast, Co. Antrim.
'I am Ulster, my people an abrupt people
Who like the spiky consonants in speech.'

59 Crown Bar, Belfast, Co. Antrim.

60/61 Slieve League Co. Donegal.

62 Below Slieve Tooey, Co. Donegal.

63 Moville, Co. Donegal. Public house.

64/65 Greencastle, Co. Donegal. Boats and fishing nets.

66 Ulster's rich fertile soil makes for good farming country.

67 Bushmills, Co. Antrim. Turf (or peat) drying on a bog. Turf is still used throughout Ireland as fuel in power stations and in the home. All small-holders have an area of bog where they cut the turf in the summer. The cut sods are dried out on the bog then stacked into piles on the sides of the road, a common sight in the summer. Bushmills is home to one of Ireland's famous whiskeys.

68/69 Mural in Queen Street, Belfast. The painting of murals is usually done secretly; some are elaborate and most are political. If they express unacceptable themes they are painted over in a matter of hours by the security forces, disappearing forever. Recently there has been an effort to record these 'works of art' for posterity with photographers rushing out at short notice to capture one before it is destroyed.

DUBLIN

For many people, Irish and visitor alike, Dublin is their favorite city. The 'fair city' charms them with its blend of elegance and dilapidation and the friendly welcome from its inhabitants. Lying at the head of Dublin Bay, it is sheltered by Howth peninsula to the north and the rocky coastline round past Dun Laoghaire to Dalkey to the south. Dublin's situation half way down the east coast of Ireland accounts for its strategic importance in more than a thousand years of Irish history; as the seat of Ireland's national government it continues to oversee Ireland's significant moments.

The name Dublin is an English one, derived from the Irish *Dubh Linn* meaning 'dark pool'; more recently the Irish name of *Baile Átha Cliath* ('the town of the hurdle ford') has been associated with the city. This name alludes to the River Liffey which divides the city in two. Rising in the lush countryside southwest of Dublin, it flows into the city through the green acres of Phoenix Park under the contrasting shadows of the Guinness brewery and Christchurch Cathedral, past the elegant Georgian façades, memories of English Protestant domination, of the Four Courts and the Custom House, and out to the Irish Sea.

Ireland's situation on the 'world's edge' of the Atlantic Ocean has seen Dublin subject to invasion and subjection by foreign powers from the Vikings in the ninth century through the Normans in the twelfth to the English in the sixteenth. In spite of, and occasionally because of, these foreign influences, Dublin has always enjoyed a strong cultural life. Trinity College has been a seat of learning since the sixteenth century and it houses the world-famous Book of Kells, an exquisite illuminated manuscript of around AD 800 which testifies to the civilization of the country before the invaders came. With political liberation in the twentieth century has come an artistic renaissance as writers and artists such as W B Yeats, James Joyce, Sean O'Casey and Flann O'Brien have rediscovered the ideas and language of their own land.

One of Dublin's principal attractions as a city to live in and visit is its compactness. Although it is home to around one third of the Republic's inhabitants, a morning's stroll can take one from O'Connell Street across the delicate Halfpenny Bridge down through the cobbled courts of Trinity College and into bustling Grafton Street. And to recover from this the quiet and contemplative may relax on leafy St Stephen's Green, while the more convivial can enjoy a glass of Guinness or whiskey in one of Dublin's many bars, meeting places for business, gossip, poetry and evenings of traditional Irish music.

71 Christ Church Dublin. The Cathedral was founded in about 1038 probably on the site of an earlier Celtic foundation. The church has many historical associations: in 1394 Richard II of England sat here in state and received homage from the Kings of the four provinces of Ireland. Here on his way to defeat at the battle of the Boyne, King James II assisted at Mass. Here also King William of Orange gave thanks for his victory there.

72 St Patricks Day Parade, Dublin. Perhaps not quite as large as the New York or Boston versions, this high-spirited and unique occasion sees visiting contingents and bands from all the corners of the globe where the Irish have settled.

73 Traditional shopfronts. Dublin. Quite a few of the most eccentric shopfronts have disappeared from the capital. They can still be found in the smaller towns and villages. Often the strangest sight for the visitor is the bar-grocery where a grocery shop has a fully stocked bar on one side.

74/75 Merrion Square, Dublin, one of Dublin's elegant Georgian squares. There are many Georgian houses and terraces in Dublin, lending the city a characteristic feel and a unique elegance.

76 St Patrick's Cathedral, Dublin. Legend has it that St Patrick baptized converts at a well on the site of this church – thus the well became a Holy well in the Christian tradition – but there is evidence to suggest that the well had pre-Christian significance. The position of the Holy Well was discovered during excavations in 1901 when a granite stone marked with an ancient Celtic cross was uncovered near the west tower.

77 O'Connell Street shrine, Dublin. On the mountains or in Ireland's best-known shopping street, there's no escape from the devout.

77

78 A flower vendor in Mary Street, Dublin. Their ringing voices preceding them, Dublin's street vendors speak a language that is half-sung and indecipherable, but they always have bargains, wit and laughter.

79 Trade Horse owners at the Royal Dublin Society Horse Show.

82/83 Phoenix Park, Dublin. The central part of this extensive park was formed by the Duke of Ormonde from the confiscated demense of the Knights Hospitallers at Killmainham. Development and planting began in 1740. It contains nearly 2000 acres, planted with beautiful trees and has a broad drive running straight for two miles between the main entrance near Kingsbridge, to the Castlenock Gate.

84/85 Phoenix Park in the winter. The Phoenix Park has herd of deer roaming through the trees and also houses the Dublin Zoological Gardens. The name of the park has the usual confused etymological history: the old name for the fields that now make up the park was Fionn usige (clear stream); this was taken to be the Irish word for phoenix.

86 Cleary's Pub, Parkgate Street, Dublin. A traditional Dublin pub, there is truth in the mythology that you can walk into a pub in Ireland and find yourself in a philosophical, policital or religious discussion when half-way through your first drink. The Irish love to talk, and better still to argue and above all to make friends.

87 Wrenboys. On the day after Christmas, known in Ireland as St Stephen's Day, the cruel tradition of the wren is still carried out over much of the country. A wren is caught, put into a glass jar and carried around by children who chant: 'The wren, the wren, the King of all Birds.' Money is given to the fiends, usually to procure the release of the unfortunate captive.

LEINSTER

Compared to the wild drama of the Munster landscape, Leinster presents a much softer contrast. With its easily accessible and fertile land, Leinster has always been one of the more populated and prosperous areas of Ireland. Its gentle east coast has many miles of golden beaches, and County Wexford is said to be the sunniest county in all Ireland. Northern and central counties such as Louth, Meath, Westmeath, and Longford are relatively flat, and in north Kildare and Offaly a vast area of bogland stretches to the River Shannon. But Leinster is not without its more rugged aspect, with the peat-covered granite domes of the Wicklow Mountains rising to the south of Dublin.

Leinster's accessibility has brought many visitors to this part of Ireland, some more welcome than others. In AD 432 St Patrick landed at the mouth of the River Boyne in County Louth, bringing Christianity to Ireland. The long history of Christianity in Ireland has left many of its most ancient monuments in Leinster. The monastery of St Ciaran at Clonmacnoise in County Offaly was founded in the sixth century and as one of the holiest places in Ireland became the burial place of the High Kings of Ireland. Leinster was the site also of the battles which in the eleventh century saw the expulsion of the Vikings from Ireland only to see the arrival of the Anglo-Normans in the twelfth. These invaders, unlike later arrivals, mixed with the native population and in many cases became 'more Irish than the Irish.' Later Protestant English settlers favored Leinster for its gentle countryside and proximity to Dublin and built many fine country houses and parks here in the eighteenth century.

Leinster today maintains many of its traditional pursuits. The Curragh at Kildare is home to Ireland's most important horse race, the Irish Sweeps Derby, and nearby is the Irish National Stud. This was founded by an Englishman in the early 1900s who studied the astrological horoscopes of his foals to decide whether to keep or sell them. Further south is Kilkenny, the 'marble city' and home to another national sport, hurling. Similar to Gaelic football, hurling has a 2000-year history and devotees regard it as an art, maintaining that 'hurling is a game for piano tuners, football is a game for piano removers.'

89 Wicklow peat and sphagnum mosses.

90/91 Enniscorthy, Co. Wexford.

92 The Curragh, Budweiser 1989.

93 Horse Racing at the Curragh. The race course at the Curragh dates from pre-Christian times: curragh is the Irish word for racecourse. The Irish Derby is run every June and this is the center of the Irish racing world.

94/95 Johnstown Castle, Co. Wexford, an impressive castellated mansion in lovely grounds. The building incorporates the tower of a fortress built in the thirteenth century.

96 Glenmalure, Co. Wicklow. Drained by the Avonbeg River, this deep mountain gorge is wild and very beautiful. Lugnaquilla, at a height of 3039 feet the highest point in the Wicklow mountains, overlocks the valley which is interesting to geologists because of two moraines formed during the glacial period. Glenmalure was often used over the years by Irish rebels; the approaches are easily defended and extremely arduous to complete.

97 Mountain sheep, Co. Wicklow.

98 Dunleer, Co. Louth. Telephone boxes and a shrine should conveniently satisfy any communication need.

99 Fall moorgrass, Co. Wicklow.

100 Gannets on Great Saltee Island, Co. Wexford.

101 Grand Canal, Inchicore. The canal stretches from Dublin to beyond the Shannon at Ballinasloe. Construction began in 1756. The canal traverses the central plain of Ireland and together with its branches is 150 miles long. It is no longer used commercially, but stretches of it are still navigable.

102 At the mart at Blessington, Co. Wicklow.

103 County Wicklow stream. Water is always
nearby in Ireland.

104 Round Tower and St. Kevin's kitchen at Glendalough, Co. Wicklow. At once the most enchanting of the glens of Wicklow and having extensive remains of an early Irish Monastery, Glendalough must be visited by any serious visitor to Ireland. St Kevin came here in the sixth century to live the life of a hermit, first in a tree on the north side of the Upper Lake, afterwards in a cave on the south side, a place that could only be reached by boat. Followers, attracted by his reputation, were numerous and a Church was built to fulfill their needs. Later, when his followers were more numerous, he founded a monastery which flourished, despite repeated attack by the Norsemen, for six centuries. The Round Tower is 103 ft high and 52 ft in circumference. It has five stories, each with one window and under the capstone four windows facing the cardinal points of a compass. St Kevin's kitchen is a double vaulted oratory with a pitched stone roof.

105 A thatched cottage at Curraloe, Co. Wexford.

MUNSTER

The province of Munster in the southwest has some of the finest scenery in the country. Its extensive coastline runs along the edge of counties Waterford, Cork, Kerry, Limerick and Clare. Tipperary is the only one of the counties not to have a coastline, and the rest of Munster is ringed by a variety of sandy coves, rocky headlands, mountains, cliffs and estuaries that draw visitors to the beauties of Bantry Bay, the Ring of Kerry and the Beara Peninsula. In Munster this rugged beauty extends inland, for the many mountain ranges mean that horizons always seem quite close. The euphoniously named Macgillycuddy's Reeks near the Killarney Lakes culminate in the lofty Carrauntuohill, at 3400 feet, Ireland's highest peak. During the Ice Age, Munster's many mountains were cut through by glaciers to form the characteristic 'gaps,' including the famous Gap of Dunloe near Killarney.

Some of Ireland's most ancient historical remains are to be found in Munster. Near Glandore, a pretty harbor village in Cork, stand the 17 stones of Drombeg, a Megalithic stone circle many thousands of years old. The remoteness created by Munster's ragged coastline attracted Christian monks from the earliest times, and Munster contains the largest number of their distinctive beehive huts, dry-built stone structures with roofs perfectly balanced without the aid of mortar. But Munster is also the site of a much more ostentatious monument to both Irish Christianity and monarchy. The Rock of Cashel in Tipperary was home to the Kings of Ireland from the fifth to the eleventh century when it became a great episcopal center. Today its unique collection of ancient buildings rises out of the Golden Vale of Tipperary to delight the unsuspecting traveller, both by day and silhouetted by night.

Munster's varied landscape and climate mean that it is home to unique variety of flora and fauna. The passing Gulf Stream has encouraged the growth of subtropical plants, while to the north, on the Burren, a weird moonscape of limestone pavements in County Clare, are found Alpine-Arctic flora, a relic of the Ice Age. But Munster is not exclusively a rural province. The city of Cork is today a prosperous urban center, with its picturesque canals and bridges, while Waterford to the east is home to the world-renowned glassmaking industry dating from 1783. Whereas the many coastal settlements provide a base for sea fishing, in the past they were safe havens for pirates, intent upon the cargoes of the passing East India Fleet. All in all, this region of surprising contrasts and great beauty never fails to provide interest and visual satisfaction.

107 Torc Waterfall, Co. Kerry. Torc mountain in the heart of the Ring of Kerry. Killarney is often described as the Reflex of Heaven.

108 Traditional Fair at Kenmare, Co. Kerry.

109 Daniel O'Connell's house at Derrynane Co.
Kerry. O'Connell elected MP for Clare in 1823
caused the crisis that led to Catholic emancipa-
tion. Throughout his long and successful Parlia-
mentary career he initiated much radical legisla-
tion. He was eventually betrayed by his faith in
legal reform.

110 Traditional horse fair at Buttevant, Co. Cork.

111 Gap of Dunloe, Co. Kerry, on the eastern side of the Macgillycuddy Reeks, Ireland's highest mountain range. In the past this journey was usually made on foot or on donkey, and many visitors to this extraordinary area still make the journey by jaunting car. Killarney is an area long eulogized by poets and travellers alike; Wordsworth, Tennyson and Thackeray all visited here and fell under its spell.

112 Little Skellig Island. The word skellig means rock-splinter. The three Skellig Islands lie in the open Atlantic 20 miles south of the Blasket Islands and 8 miles from the coast. Travelers usually start from Knightstown on Valentia Island, where there is a boat service. It is a perfect excursion for the lover of cliff scenery and the archaeologist. Landing on the island is tricky in bad weather because there is no shelter.

113 Near Loop head, Co. Clare.

114 Coomasaharn Lake, near Glenbeigh, Co. Kerry.

115 Bee hive monks' hut at Skellig Michael monastery, Co. Kerry. This is the largest of the three Skellig islands, a mass of precipitous slate rock a half a mile by a quarter. There is a light-house here and a good harbor from which there is a road to the plateau where these huts are to be found. There are five huts or clochans in all, with corbelled roofs. Beside them is a tiny oratory of similar construction. On a lower level there is a sixth hut, a second oratory and cross slabs. The huts have six feet thick walls and contain cup-boards. An almost frost-free atmosphere has ensured their excellent condition. The monastery was plundered by the Vikings in the ninth Century, but continued until the monks moved to the main-land at Ballinskellig in the twelfth Century. On a fine day the view from this plateau over the Kerry coastline is breathtaking.

116 At Inagh, Co. Clare, a man makes hay.

117 Traditional cottage at Ballyvaughan, Co.
Clare.

118 An extraordinary pattern is formed by lobster pots on Valentia Island, Co. Kerry. This island is a popular resort and deep-sea fishing is available; there is an excellent harbor. The cliffs at Bray head offer spectacular views of the coast of Dingle.

119 On the Burren, Co. Clare, a sighting of Bloody Cranesbill, Geranium Sanguinem. Many Alpine flowers grow in this strange and lonely place.

120/121 Dingle town and harbor, Co. Kerry.

122 The Rock of Cashel, Co. Tipperary. This dramatic sight rising steeply above the surrounding countryside of Co. Tipperary, was a fifth century seat of the pre-Christian kings of Munster, the most famous of whom was Brian Boru, crowned here in 977. It is said that it was in this Castle St Patrick preached using the shamrock to illustrate the threefold nature of the Christian trinity. The ruins date from the Christian era when Cashel became an important ecclesiastical center.

123 Driving to Doolin, Co. Clare. Doolin, a coastal town is reached by means of winding roads with spectacular views of the Atlantic. It is a well-known center for Irish Traditional musicians. In the pubs in Doolin there are impromptu 'sessions' every night with fiddles, tins whistles, and bodhrans (pronounced bow rawns) providing energetic music. Appetites, whetted no doubt by the crashing ocean outside, find the Guinness here tastes better than it ever should.

124 A view of the Franciscan Quin Abbey, Co. Clare, showing the dormitcries and cloisters.

125 Bog holes in Co. Clare.
'Cold is the night in the Great Bog, a terrible rain-
storm beats down; a deep song at which the clear
wind laughs screams over the shelter of the
wood.'
Translated from the Irish, twelfth century.

126 *A majestic Galway Hooker at Kinvara, Co. Clare. The hooker was the sea-fishing boat peculiar to the west of Ireland. There is a festival in Kinvara in late summer which celebrates these boats.*

127 *The Cliffs of Moher County Clare.*
A rocky promontory, looking on
the coiling surface of the sea
To see the waves, crest on crest
of the great shining ocean, composing
a hymn to the creator, without rest
To hear the whisper of small waves
against the rocks, that endless sea-
sound, like keening over graves.
St Colmcille; version by John Montague

*128 Fields near the Burren, Co. Clare, from which
a meager living is eked out.*